MISSION

AMSTERDAM

Author: Catherine Aragon
Designer: Nada Orlić

MISSION LOCATION:
AMSTERDAM

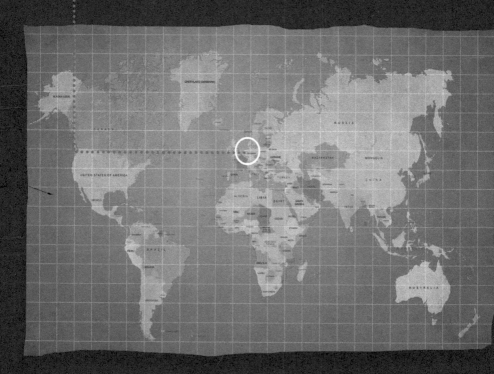

CONTENTS

AFTER COMPLETING EACH MISSION, CHECK (√) THE BOX AND WRITE THE NUMBER OF POINTS EARNED.

AT THE END, WRITE THE TOTAL NUMBER OF POINTS HERE:

ATTENTION: FUTURE SPECIAL AGENTS <u>YOU</u>
AND <u>CASE OFFICERS</u> <u>GROWNUPS</u>

CONGRATULATIONS! THE SIA (SECRET INTERNATIONAL AGENCY) HAS SELECTED YOU AS A CANDIDATE TO BECOME A SPECIAL AGENT.

The SIA carries out important assignments, secretly collecting intelligence in all corners of the globe. ("Intelligence" is spy-speak for "information.") Currently, we are in dire need of agents. Many want to join us, but only a few have what it takes.

HOW WILL YOU PROVE YOU'RE READY TO JOIN THE MOST ELITE SPY AGENCY IN THE WORLD? You must complete a series of missions in Amsterdam. Similar to a scavenger hunt (only better), these missions will require you to carry out challenging investigations and collect valuable intel (short for "intelligence"). For each mission, you'll earn points towards becoming a special agent.

YOUR ASSIGNMENT: TRAVEL TO AMSTERDAM WITH YOUR TEAM, LED BY YOUR CASE OFFICER. (A case officer accompanies agents on missions. Your case officer is your parent or other trusted adult.) You must earn at least 200 points to become a SIA special agent.

-The mission list and mission scorecard are on page 1.

-Read the "Anytime Missions" early, so that you'll remain on alert and ready to earn points. You can complete these at any time during your stay.

-You don't need to complete all of the missions to reach 200 points or complete them in any particular order.

BONUS MISSION

Want even more Amsterdam fun? Visit **scavengerhuntadventures.com/bonus** (all lowercase) today to download your **free bonus mission: "MINT TOWER."**

(Plus, you'll get *The Museum Spy*, our free e-book!)

"Get Your Bonus Mission Today!"

MISSION RULES

- Be kind and respectful to team members.

- Your case officer (your parent or other trusted adult) has the final decision regarding point awards.

- Your case officer serves as the official "scorekeeper."

- Your case officer has the final decision on what missions will be attempted. (Don't worry, you can still earn enough points to become an agent without completing all the missions.)

- Always be on alert. You never know when a chance to earn points lies just around the corner.

TO CONCEAL THEIR REAL IDENTITIES, SPECIAL AGENTS ALWAYS USE CODE NAMES. FOR EXAMPLE, JAMES BOND'S CODE NAME IS 007. THINK OF YOUR OWN CODE NAME TO USE DURING YOUR MISSION IN AMSTERDAM.

SIGN YOUR CODE NAME HERE:

ALPHA .

21 / 09 / 19

DATE

Important: For the missions you will need a pen or pencil and a camera. **LET THE MISSIONS BEGIN — GOOD LUCK!**

WESTERN EUROPE

IT'S CRITICAL THAT AGENTS HAVE A "LAY OF THE LAND" BEFORE SETTING OUT ON MISSIONS. USE THIS BRIEF TO GET FAMILIAR WITH YOUR MISSION LOCATION BEFORE ARRIVAL.

Mission location: the city of Amsterdam (red dot) in the Netherlands (dark red), a country bordered by Belgium and Germany.

North
Sea

AMSTERDAM
The Hague
Rotterdam

NETHERLANDS

Official Country Name: the Netherlands; (known as "Nederland" in Dutch) people also call it Holland
Language: Dutch (known as "Nederlands" in Dutch)
Capitals: Amsterdam (official), The Hague (seat of government)
Currency: Euro
Netherlands Population: 16.8 million
Amsterdam Population: 800,000

EUROS

FLAG

RIJKSMUSEUM

("Rikes Museum") *(State Museum)*

ALL THE SPY GEAR AND TOP SECRET INTEL IN THE WORLD WON'T HELP YOU IF YOU DON'T HAVE SHARP EYES AND A MIND LIKE A STEEL TRAP. LET'S TEST YOUR SKILLS IN THIS MUSEUM.

☐ AS YOU EXPLORE THE MUSEUM, HUNT DOWN PAINTINGS OF KIDS YOUR AGE.
   (ONE POINT PER PAINTING, TEN POINTS MAX)

1
POINT
EACH

☐ BONUS: REPORT TO YOUR CASE OFFICER IN WHAT YEAR THE PAINTING WAS CREATED.
   (TEN POINTS MAX)

1
POINT
EACH

47

TOTAL POINTS

- KIDS IN PAINTINGS
- PAINTINGS' YEARS
- CHARLES V'S SEAL
- JAVANESE MEN
- WILLIAM OF ORANGE
- DUTCH EAST INDIA COMPANY
- NIGHT WATCH ARTIST
- DANCING ANIMAL
- THE MERRY FAMILY
- DOLLHOUSES

☐ **FIND THIS SEAL OF THE GREAT RULER CHARLES V* HIDDEN IN A TAPESTRY.***

2 POINTS

The color will be quite different, as the tapestry has faded through the centuries. But you should still be able to match the double-headed eagle as well as the shield in the middle, which has small castles in the upper left.

Charles V was destined for greatness since the day he inherited the Netherlands in the 1500's at the age of <u>six</u>. (Charles' aunt actually controlled his kingdom until he grew a bit older.)

An ambitious young man, Charles V controlled lands far beyond the Netherlands. He eventually became the most powerful person in all of Europe, ruling lands as far away as South and Central America, which Spain (a country he ruled) colonized. For all that he achieved, he claimed the title "emperor."

Charles V, as a young man

*(V=5 in Roman numerals; Charles V = Charles the Fifth)

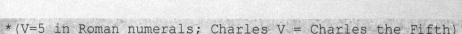

*tapestry = a heavy cloth with woven designs that's used as a wall hanging

7

Find the paintings of these five men, from the island of Java, Indonesia, a land the Dutch once controlled. To make this clue a bit of a challenge, we've switched the paintings' tops and bottoms.

☐ **ANALYZE THE PAINTINGS AND MATCH UP THE LETTERS ON THE PAINTINGS' TOPS WITH THE NUMBERS ON THE PAINTINGS' BOTTOMS.**

5 POINTS

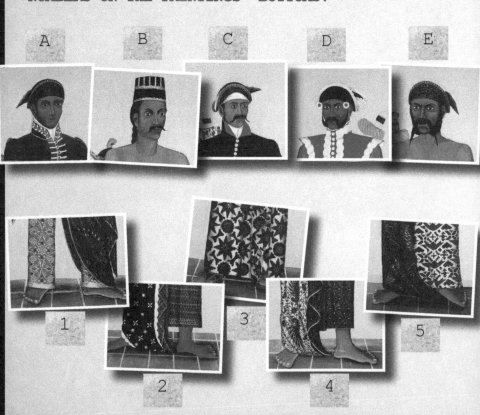

☐ **TRACK DOWN THIS PAINTING OF WILLIAM OF ORANGE, A.K.A. THE "FATHER" OF THE NETHERLANDS.**

2 POINTS

This man has at least three titles: the two above plus William the Silent (due to his quiet nature). He was named the "father" of the Netherlands because he led an uprising against the Spanish, who, in the 1500's, controlled Holland. This would lead to Holland saying "adios" to Spain and eventually claiming its independence.

He became a prince at the age of 11, when he inherited territory in the Netherlands and France (including the small French kingdom of "Orange"). William was one of 12 children – imagine having four brothers and seven sisters!

the young prince

THE DUTCH EAST INDIA COMPANY

Poking around in your kitchen at home, eventually you'd come across a few kinds of spices, jars of powders (or possibly seeds) used to flavor food. These spices grew in fields or on trees before being harvested, packaged, and sent to your local store and put on sale for a few dollars. No big deal.

However, back in the 1600's in Amsterdam, spices were expensive and a major "status symbol." If you wanted to impress someone, you'd invite them over and serve food with spices like pepper, nutmeg, and cloves. Europeans forked over up to 100 times what spice companies paid the growers

a spice merchant

back in Asia. Spices not only flavored food, but were thought to have healing powers.

European trading companies brought spices all the way from Asia, a land where fortune awaited in "fields of gold" (spice fields), which Europeans were hungry to take as their own.

The Dutch claimed the number one spot in the spice trade, leaving their competitors like the Portugese and English in the dust. They beat them to the famed "Spice Islands" (a.k.a. the Molucca Islands in Indonesia), the only place in the world where nutmeg and cloves grew.

the Dutch arriving in Indonesia

The spice trade hauled in so much cash that the Dutch government gave one trading company (the Dutch East India Company) powers held before only by the government: training an army, making treaties with foreign leaders, declaring war, and creating colonies; basically anything the company needed to dominate the spice trade. The company's leaders, like Gov. Coen, stopped

Governor Coen, founder of the company HQ in Indonesia

at nothing to stay on top: they burned competitor crops and killed other spice traders.

Ever heard the saying, "what goes around comes around?" The company may have made tons of money in the 1600's, but by the late 1700's it had too many problems to count and soon went out of business. In its heyday, however, the company had a trade network spread from present-day South Africa, Iran, India, Japan, China, to Indonesia.

Locate the below painting of a trade post in India.

☐ **FIND THE PAINTING'S YEAR PAINTED ON THE CANVAS.** **2** POINTS

☐ **HOW MANY DUTCH FLAGS CAN YOU FIND IN IT?** **4** POINTS
(We found 15 - try to top our count!)

the artist

Hunt down the museum's most famous painting, *Night Watch*. Here, the man in black (a city police captain) orders the man on the right to get the guardsmen ready and marching.

☐ **WHAT'S THE NAME OF THE PAINTING'S ARTIST?**

2 POINTS

Locate the painting with these kids.

☐ **WHAT ANIMAL ARE THE KIDS TEACHING TO DANCE?**

2 POINTS

Find the painting on the next page, correctly named *The Merry Family*. Compare the painting you find to the copy on the next page.

 WHAT FIVE THINGS HAVE BEEN ADDED TO THIS COPY THAT DON'T APPEAR IN THE ORIGINAL?

5 POINTS

Locate the collection of antique dollhouses. Not your every-day dollhouses, don't even think about playing with these "toys!" These are centuries-old models of homes of wealthy Amsterdam residents, complete with wooden furniture, dishes, and silverware.

 IN YOUR OPINION WHAT HOUSEHOLD ITEMS ARE MISSING FROM THE DOLLHOUSES THAT COULD HAVE APPEARED IN OLD AMSTERDAM HOUSES?

3 POINTS

VAN GOGH MUSEUM

(Van Gogh = "Van Go")

Vincent, around age 13

Theo Van Gogh

Vincent's self-portrait

AGENTS MUST HAVE FIRST-RATE ABILITIES WHEN IT COMES TO ANALYZING IMAGES, SUCH AS PAINTINGS, IN ORDER TO GATHER IMPORTANT INTEL. TIME TO TEST YOUR SKILLS IN AMSTERDAM'S MOST FAMOUS MUSEUM.

Vincent Van Gogh's family had a long history in the art world: three men in his family were art dealers. His brother, Theo, also followed his family's lead to become an art dealer. Vincent tried selling art too, but eventually chose instead to create art as a painter. As an art dealer Theo gave Vincent advice all the time about his painting style. Vincent trusted and depended on Theo's guidance.

- VAN GOGH'S DARKEST AND BRIGHTEST WORKS
- VAN GOGH SELFIES
- MYSTERY BOOK
- POTATO PAINTING
- SUNFLOWERS
- GAUGUIN'S PAINTING
- BEDROOM PAINTING
- HOLLAND'S 2ND CAPITAL
- VAN GOGH'S APARTMENT BUILDING
- YOUR COLLECTION CHOICES

Following Vincent's death in the late 1800's, people grew to appreciate his paintings, and today they're worth millions of dollars. When Vincent was alive though, he was an unknown struggling artist, dependent on his brother for money as well.

Many of Vincent's earlier paintings are quite dark and gloomy, painted with various shades of grey, brown, and black. Theo advised his brother to liven up his creations. As you wander around the museum, stay on point and examine the colors (or lack of colors) in Vincent's many paintings. Find the paintings' descriptions beside the works and note the year Vincent created them.

☐ **WHAT ARE THE YEARS OF THE DARKEST VAN GOGH PAINTINGS YOU FIND?**

3 POINTS

☐ **WHAT ARE THE YEARS OF THE BRIGHTEST VAN GOGH PAINTINGS YOU FIND?**

3 POINTS

☐ **DID VINCENT TAKE THEO'S ADVICE AND BRIGHTEN HIS PAINTINGS?**
(Are the newer paintings generally brighter and more colorful compared to the older ones?)

3 POINTS

my notes:

....

....

Van Gogh took quite a fancy to painting...Van Gogh. (If he lived today his cell phone probably would be full of "selfies.") He was also too poor to afford to pay models to pose for paintings.

☐ **FIND VAN GOGH'S "SELFIES" (SELF-PORTRAITS).** **10 POINTS MAX**

2
POINTS
EACH

• • Track down this book in a painting.

☐ **WHAT BOOK IS IT?**

2
POINTS

Van Gogh's father, a minister, owned this book. Van Gogh chose to include one his favorite books, *La Joie de Vivre* ("Lah Jwah duh Veev") (a French term for "The Joy of Life") next to his father's book as a bit of a poke at his dad. (The two were often at odds with each other.)

Locate this man, enjoying the "fruits of his labor" (potatoes) after a long day in the fields.

☐ **WHAT IS THE NAME OF THIS PAINTING?**

☐ **HOW MANY PEOPLE ARE WITH HIM?**

my notes:

_____

_____

A

B

C

D

Van Gogh created a series of sunflower paintings
to share with his friend and fellow painter Paul
Gauguin ("Go-gan"). Paintings from the sunflower
series hang in various museums and private
collections around the world. Only one of the four
above actually hangs in the Van Gogh Museum.

☐ WHICH ONE OF THESE HANGS IN THE MUSEUM?

3
POINTS

☐ BONUS: ONCE YOU LOCATE IT, FIND 'VINCENT'
PAINTED ON THE CANVAS.

1
POINT

☐ **BEFORE LEAVING THE MUSEUM, TRACK DOWN THIS PAINTING GAUGUIN CREATED OF HIS BUDDY, VAN GOGH, WORKING ON SUNFLOWERS.**

2 POINTS

Paul Gauguin

Track down one of Van Gogh's most famous paintings, *The Bedroom*, (his bedroom). Now that you've had practice analyzing art, it's time for a challenge! If you can complete this clue, you truly have what it takes to be a special agent!

☐ **FIND THREE OBJECTS ADDED TO THE COPY ABOVE WHICH DON'T APPEAR IN THE ORIGINAL PAINTING.**

3
POINTS

my notes:

This painting, by French artist Claude Monet ("Monay"), contains three symbols of Holland: tulips, windmills, and boats. It's a scene near one of Holland's two capitals. Amsterdam is considered Holland's official capital. However, the Dutch Parliament and Supreme Court rest in this city.

☐ **HUNT DOWN THIS PAINTING. WHAT'S THE PAINTING'S NAME?**

2 POINTS

☐ **LOCATE THIS BUILDING IN A PAINTING.**

2 POINTS

Van Gogh lived in this green-shuttered structure, and he'd eat at the café in the painting. He created this in 1888, after he'd moved to the South of France, a land filled with sun and bright colors, perfect for painting.

☐ **IF YOU WERE AN ART COLLECTOR, WHICH THREE PAINTINGS IN THE MUSEUM WOULD YOU WANT TO ADD TO YOUR COLLECTION?**

3 POINTS

VONDELPARK

VONDELPARK MAP
(EASTERN SECTION)

N

VONDEL STATUE

MAIN ENTRANCE*

PICASSO SCULPTURE

*Main Entrance by the street "Stadhouderskade"

("Stahd-how-der-skahd-eh")

SPECIAL AGENTS MUST HAVE TOP-NOTCH SKILLS WHEN IT COMES TO ANALYZING MAPS.

☐ LOCATE THE GATE WITH THE PARK'S NAME AT THE MAIN ENTRANCE.

2 POINTS

12

TOTAL POINTS

☐ **TRACK DOWN THE STATUE OF THE MAN FOR WHOM THE PARK IS NAMED, JOOST VAN DEN VONDEL*.**

2 POINTS

Vondel

(*"Yoast vahn den Vondel")

Vondel was a writer, and here's a piece of related "intel" to assist in your search:

In the statue, Vondel holds a book in one hand and a feather in the other.

☐ **FIND 'AMSTERDAM' IN GOLD ON THE STATUE.**

1 POINT

my notes:

Vondel's Resting Place

Vondel died in 1679, making it all the way to the age of 91 (quite an accomplishment, especially back in those days).

☐ **FIND THE NAME OF THE AMSTERDAM MONUMENT WHERE HE'S BURIED SOMEWHERE ON THE STATUE.**

2 POINTS

Hint: The resting place has the initials N.K. (a monument also mentioned in your book).

☐ **LOCATE THE ABSTRACT SCULPTURE BY SPANISH ARTIST PABLO PICASSO.**

2 POINTS

The name of the sculpture: *The Fish*.

Picasso

☐ **FIND THREE ITEMS ADDED TO THIS PHOTO WHICH DO NOT APPEAR IN THE ORIGINAL SCULPTURE.**

3 POINTS

BEGIJNHOF

("Beh-hine-hof")

Begijnhof gets its name from the "beguines," ("beh-gheens") a group of women who led lives similar to nuns and worshipped at a chapel in this square.

☐ **TRACK DOWN THE ENTRANCE TO THE GROUP'S "HIDDEN" CHAPEL, THE BEGIJNHOF KAPEL.**
(Kapel = "kah-pell")

2 POINTS

Hint: The address is Begijnhof 30, so keep a lookout for building numbers.

☐ **FIND THE BEGUINE STATUE.**

2 POINTS

10

- HIDDEN CHAPEL
- BEGUINE STATUE
- CHURCH SHEPHERD
- CHURCH YEAR
- OLDEST WOODEN HOUSE

TOTAL POINTS

☐ **LOCATE THIS MAN WITH HIS SHEEP, LOOKING OUT OVER THE SQUARE.**

 2 *POINTS*

For centuries, this English church has held services here, stopping only during World War II when the Nazis took control of Amsterdam.

☐ **WHAT YEAR IS CARVED ON THE CHURCH?**

 2 *POINTS*

☐ **FIND THIS WORD PAINTED ON A BUILDING.**

2 *POINTS* 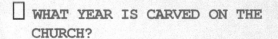 **houten**

Note: The "h" will appear a bit fancier on the building.

Houten ('how-teh') = wooden. This 550-year-old structure is the oldest wooden house in the country. Wooden houses this old are few and far between. Whoever built this place was quite brave with their building material choice. In the 1400's Amsterdam suffered from two massive fires, with 75% of the city destroyed. Following these tragedies, residents were ordered to build their homes with fire-resistant brick, clay, or stone. Lucky for the "Houten Huis" residents (Huis = House), this house has managed to stand for over 500 years.

DE DAM

("Deh Dahm")

AGENTS MUST HAVE A KEEN EYE FOR DETAIL. THEY ALWAYS NEED TO HAVE THEIR EYES PEELED FOR THE TINIEST CLUES – CRITICAL INFORMATION THAT OTHERS OFTEN MISS. TIME TO PUT YOUR SKILLS TO THE TEST.

Welcome to De Dam ("Dam Square"), the heart of Amsterdam. Here the small village of "Aemstelledamme" ("Ahmstel-eh Dahm-eh") was founded around 1270, named after a dam built for the Amstel River. Three important monuments now stand here, the site of your next mission.

34+

TOTAL POINTS

- GOLD SHIP
- SKELETONS & SKULLS
- CHANDELIERS
- OLD MAP
- CELESTIAL GLOBE
- KIDS IN PAINTINGS

- TROMPE L'OEIL
- DE DAM PAINTING
- NIEUWE KERK & SUNDIAL
- NATIONAAL MONUMENT'S YEARS, SCULPTURES, URNS

#1: KONINKLIJK PALEIS

("Ko-nin-klik Pah-lays")
(Royal Palace)

Before you rests the royal palace of the king of the Netherlands, King Willem Alexander. Even though this is the king's palace, he and his family don't actually live here. (They live about an hour away in a suburb of the Netherland's seat of government, The Hague.) The Dutch use this place for special events. If there's an event or if the king's in town, the palace closes its doors to tourists. (If the palace is closed, use your 'Anytime Missions' to make up points.)

The King with Queen Maxima and Princesses Catharina-Amalia, Ariane, and Alexia

The King (left) at age 14 with his brother

☐ **BEFORE VENTURING INSIDE, TRACK DOWN A GOLD SHIP SOMEWHERE ON THE PALACE EXTERIOR.**

2
POINTS

As you explore the palace, remain on the lookout for skeletons and skulls lurking about.

HUNT DOWN:

☐ A SKELETON TAKING A BREAK, APPEARING DEEP IN THOUGHT

2 POINTS

☐ A SKULL WHO HAS UPSET SOME BABIES

2 POINTS

According to our reports about the palace, 51 chandeliers ("shan-duh-leers") decorate the interior section open to the public. As you wander around, keep count of the chandeliers you spot.

5 POINTS

☐ REPORT TO YOUR CASE OFFICER WHETHER THIS COUNT (51) IS CURRENTLY CORRECT.

my notes:

☐ **LOCATE THIS MAP.** **2** POINTS

☐ **FIND THE NETHERLANDS ON IT.** **1** POINT

Europe will be labelled 'Europa' on the map. (In Latin, the language of Ancient Rome, Europa = Europe.)

☐ **TRACK DOWN THIS "GLOBE."** **2** POINTS

This is not a regular globe that shows the world, but a "celestial" globe, displaying the planets, stars, and constellations. Back in the 1600's the Dutch battled other European nations to rule the high seas, with the winner claiming the title "world's most powerful country." The Dutch, of course, believed Amsterdam was the world's most important city. Since Amsterdam was the most important city on Earth, then Amsterdam was no doubt the center of the universe. This sculpture represents that belief.

Inside the palace rooms hang portraits of Holland's royal family and other important figures. Although these paintings often include only adults, you'll also find some kids in the paintings.

___ **POINTS FOR EVERY PAINTING OF A SCHOOL-AGE KID (BETWEEN AGES 5 AND 18, APPROXIMATELY)**

(Your case officer sets the number of points per painting, as sometimes a few palace rooms can be closed for repairs.)

The Palace & Dam Square, around 1890

At one time the Royal Palace served as Amsterdam's town hall and seat of the city's treasurer. Hopefully Amsterdam's treasurers kept neater records than those shown in this painting, *Treasurer's Papers and Documents*.

☐ **TRACK DOWN THE ABOVE PAINTING.**

2 POINTS

The artist created it using what's called a "trompe l'oeil" ("tromp loy") effect. This is French for "trick the eye." Objects in "trompe l'oeil" paintings are meant to appear as if they're real, in 3-D.

☐ **IN YOUR OPINION, DID THE ARTIST SUCCEED IN PAINTING THE PAPERS SO THEY APPEAR REAL AND IN 3-D?**

2 POINTS

AFBEELDING van den DAM, het STADHUYS, de NIEUWE-KERCK, de WAAG, en de OUDE-KERCKS-TOOREN van AMSTERDAM

#2: NIEUWE KERK *("New Kairk") (New Church)*

Examine the above painting of Dam Square, created at the very end of the 1600's, with the Royal Palace on the left.

SPOT: **1 POINT EACH**

☐ THE GOLD SHIP YOU FOUND ATOP
   THE ROYAL PALACE

☐ AMSTERDAM'S COAT OF ARMS

☐ "NIEUWE KERK" ("NEW KAIRK")
   WRITTEN ON THE PAINTING

The Nieuwe Kerk has this set of windows.

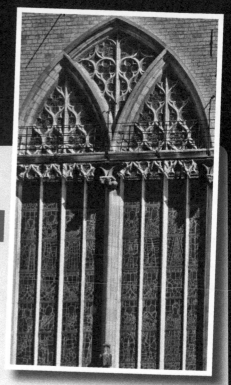

☐ **USING THE PAINTING AND THIS PHOTO, TRACK DOWN THE LOCATION OF THE NIEUWE KERK ON THE SQUARE.** **2** *POINTS*

The "new church" is actually quite old: over 600 years. Dutch royalty, heads of state, and other important figures have been sworn into office, married, and buried at this site.

Your mission here only takes place outside.

☐ **FIND THE OLD-FASHIONED CLOCK, A.K.A. SUNDIAL.** **2** *POINTS*

my notes:

Allied troops march
through Holland in WW II

#3: NATIONAAL MONUMENT *("Nationaal" sounds the same as "National")*

The Dutch built this monument (an "obelisk"), to remember the victims and fighters in World War II.

World War II (WW II) lasted from 1939 to 1945. The "Allies" (led by the U.S., Great Britain, Russia, and China) battled the "Axis" (led by Germany, Japan, and Italy). The Dutch declared they would not take sides in the beginning of the war, but the Nazis ("not-zees") (the Germans) invaded their country anyway. They invaded in 1940 and held the country for five long years, until 1945.

☐ **LOCATE THE YEARS "1940 AND "1945" ON THE MONUMENT.**

2
POINTS

FIND THE SYMBOLS OF:

☐ **WAR (FOUR MEN)**

☐ **PEACE (WOMAN WITH CHILD)**

☐ **RESISTANCE (MEN WITH DOGS)**

(The Dutch fought to "resist" the Nazi control of their country.)

☐ **HOW MANY URNS DECORATE THE MONUMENT?**

These contain soil from each of the eleven provinces of the Netherlands, plus one for the Dutch East Indies (a former Dutch colony, which today is the nation of Indonesia).

Spring, 1945: Holland is finally free - let's celebrate!

ANNE FRANK HOUSE

The sign on Anne's house. Huis = House, and is pronounced "house" too.

Anne Frank, her family, and four friends spent two years hiding here, hoping to avoid capture by the Nazis, a political group who invaded and controlled Amsterdam from 1940 to 1945 during World War II.

The Nazis originally came to power in Germany in a period when the country had lots of problems following World War I (which ended in 1918). The Nazis despised Jews, and blamed Germany's problems on them, even though they weren't responsible.

Jewish families, like Anne's, fled Germany. Anne's family thought they'd be safe in Amsterdam.

The grave of Anne and her sister Margot

The blacked out windows, revolving bookcase, and "Secret Annex," however, proved not to be enough. After hiding for two years, the Franks were betrayed by someone who gave up their location, and the entire group, except Anne's father, died tragically at the hands of the Nazis.

When the war ended in 1945 and Amsterdam was finally free from the Nazis, Anne's father Otto returned home. A family friend had discovered Anne's diary, telling the story of her teenage life while in hiding. The family friend rescued Anne's diary and gave it to Anne's father upon his return. Today, Anne's diary is famous around the world for its message of hope.

As you explore Anne's house, you'll find it a small and somber place – not exactly a location suited for a scavenger hunt. While you're in Anne's house, take special note of the reminders of her family's everyday life. After your visit, think back to Anne's personal items you saw (for example her books, posters, and postcards) – simple things that brought a bit of happiness to her days inside the house.

☐ **WHAT ITEMS DO YOU HAVE IN YOUR ROOM THAT ARE SIMILAR TO THOSE IN ANNE'S ROOM?**

3
POINTS

HET SCHEEPVAARTMUSEUM

("Het Shape-vart-museum")   (National Maritime Museum)

Outside the museum: the 'Amsterdam' ship

Back in the 1600's & 1700's Dutch sailors cris-crossed the seas in ships like the *Amsterdam*, in a race against European rivals to claim lands around the globe. At one point, no country had as many ships sailing the ocean blue as the Dutch. In 1749 the crew of this vessel had their sights set on Indonesia (in Southeast Asia). Unfortunately they didn't make it far and had an accident off the coast of England. Before you stands a replica.

In those days it took around eight months to get from Amsterdam to Southeast Asia. **Could you spend months on end living in a small space like this?**

41

TOTAL POINTS

Climb aboard this vessel and have your photo snapped living the life of a Dutch sailor:

2 POINTS EACH

☐ RELAXING IN A HAMMOCK (A.K.A. YOUR BED)

☐ MANNING A CANNON

☐ SITTING IN ONE OF THE WOODEN BARRELS

☐ _____ (YOUR CHOICE OF ACTIVITY)

☐ BONUS: TAKE A PHOTO OF YOUR CASE OFFICER(S) PLAYING THE ROLE OF A DUTCH SAILOR.

3 POINTS

☐ FIND THE EMBLEM OF THE DUTCH EAST INDIA COMPANY ON THE SHIP.

2 POINTS

(VOC = Vereenigde Oostindische Compagnie = "Veren-guh Oast-in-deesh-uh Co-pah-nee") Got all that? This company owned the *Amsterdam*. See their story on page 10.

Inside the museum

Knowing directions is key for successful seafaring.

☐ **WHAT ARE THE DUTCH WORDS FOR NORTH, SOUTH, EAST, AND WEST?**

3 POINTS

To find the answer, keep a look out for the word "West" in large letters on a wall. This word is the same in Dutch and English. Use this "intel" and the compass below (with Dutch direction initials) to figure out this clue.

Old maps of the world fill this museum. Back in the days when cartographers* created some of these, parts of the globe had yet to be fully explored,

*cartographer = a person who creates maps

Volvo Ocean Race

Amsterdam Map, 1688

so the mapmakers' simply had to guess at parts of their maps' design. Track down & analyze a few old maps of the world.

☐ **IN YOUR OPINION WHICH MAP CONTAINS THE MOST ACCURATE REPRESENTATION OF THE WORLD?** **4** POINTS

☐ **TRACK DOWN OLD MAPS OF THE CITY OF AMSTERDAM. (THREE POINTS MAX)** **1** POINT EACH

Locate the display of model seafaring vessels, including boats from the 1600's to the luxury yachts of today's millionaires and billionaires.

Picture yourself back in Holland's "Golden Age," (the 1600's) when the Dutch had ships sailing to the four corners of the globe.

☐ **IF YOU HAD TO VENTURE FROM AMSTERDAM TO ASIA OR THE "NEW WORLD" BACK THEN, WHICH MODEL REPRESENTS YOUR VESSEL OF CHOICE FOR YOUR LONG VOYAGE?** **2** POINTS

Fast forward to today. Currently, the Dutch hold the record for number of wins in the Volvo Ocean Race, a round-the-world yacht race.

☐ **IF YOU WERE PART OF A CREW ENTERING SUCH A RACE AROUND THE WORLD TODAY, WHICH MODEL REPRESENTS YOUR VESSEL OF CHOICE?** **2** POINTS

☐ **ONE POINT FOR EVERY DUTCH FLAG YOU FIND IN A PAINTING.   10 POINTS MAX**

1 POINT EACH

To keep you on your toes, you can only receive one point per painting. (Some paintings will have more than one Dutch flag.)

Locate the ship decorations display.

☐ **IF YOU WERE A BOAT CAPTAIN AND HAD TO CHOOSE ONE OF THESE TO DECORATE THE VERY FRONT OF A VESSEL, WHICH ONE WOULD YOU CHOOSE?**

2
POINTS

Hunt down the display of navigational instruments.

☐ **FIND AN "ASTROLABE."**

2
POINTS

(The museum's astrolabes may not appear exactly the same as this example.)

In the days before GPS and satellites, sailors employed instruments like this one, which used the position of the sun, moon, stars, and planets, to chart their course. (A tad bit of luck also played a part in helping them find their way.)

NEMO SCIENCE CENTER

ONE OF THE MOST IMPORTANT RULES OF SPYING: BLEND IN WITH YOUR SURROUNDINGS. YOU CAN NEVER SPOT THE BEST AGENTS BECAUSE THEY DON'T *LOOK* LIKE AGENTS. HERE, THAT MEANS "PLAYING TOURIST" BY STROLLING AROUND THE MUSEUM (AND TAKING A FEW PHOTOS).

To "keep your cover" as a typical museum visitor, you must find/complete these activities inside:

☐ CHAIN REACTION DEMO

☐ "TRICK YOUR BRAIN" ROOM ILLUSION

2
POINTS
EACH

☐ SOUND WAVES (WHISPERING) EXPERIMENT

13

TOTAL POINTS

Locate the museum's chemistry lab.

☐ HAVE YOUR PHOTO TAKEN AS A CHEMIST, COMPLETE WITH A WHITE LAB COAT, READY TO CONDUCT EXPERIMENTS.

2 POINTS

Make your way up to the rooftop, with a view of Amsterdam as your reward for making it all the way.

SPOT:

☐ A "NEMO" SIGN LIKE THE ONE BELOW

2 POINTS

☐ A NETHERLANDS FLAG (3 POINTS MAX)

1 POINT EACH

KASTEEL MUIDERSLOT

("Ka-steel My-der-slowt) (Muiderslot Castle)

A royal by the name of Floris V*, who ruled Holland from the age of 12, built the original Muiderslot Castle in the 1200's. Floris' father tragically died in battle, leaving Floris with the title, "Count of Holland," when he was only two years old, barely old enough to even speak.

From the minute Floris became Count, his aunts and uncles viciously fought over which of them would claim the title of "regent." The regent chosen would basically rule Holland until Floris would "come of age" ten years later. Back then, turning 12 meant you'd achieved the age where you had the smarts to rule an entire kingdom.

Do you think you could rule over Holland at age 12?

(*V=5 in Roman numerals. 'Floris V' = 'Floris The Fifth')

24

TOTAL POINTS

- LION SYMBOL
- DRAWBRIDGE
- MOAT
- ARROW SLITS
- P.C. HOOFT RELIEF
- HOOFT & VONDEL PAINTING
- ARMOR DISPLAY
- CASTLE COSTUMES

As you explore, keep your eyes peeled for the symbol of the Count of Holland - a single lion.

☐ **ONE POINT FOR EVERY 'SINGLE LION' SYMBOL YOU FIND. 5 POINTS MAX**

1 POINT EACH

Sadly, Floris' original fortress was torn down. Then in the late 1300's Albert I ('Albert the First'), the Count of Holland at that time, rebuilt his castle on the same spot.

FLORIS V

ALBERT I

49

The key to clever castle construction: a multi-part "defense" system. Today fortresses like this may make a nice postcard image, but back then their purpose was protecting the people inside.

Confirm whether this castle has three items essential in defending it from enemies:

☐ DRAWBRIDGE **2** POINTS

☐ MOAT **2** POINTS

☐ ARROW SLITS (5 POINTS MAX) **1** POINT EACH

Not all castle residents were royalty. After the Counts, a writer named P.C. Hooft not only claimed the castle in the early 1600's, but appointed himself "sheriff" of the surrounding area.

☐ FIND THIS RELIEF OF P.C. HOOFT. **2** POINTS

☐ ONCE INSIDE, HUNT DOWN THE PAINTING AT THE TOP OF THE NEXT PAGE. **2** POINTS

HOOFT | VONDEL

The men in the center: "sheriff" Hooft and his
good friend and fellow writer, Joost van den
Vondel ("Yoast Vahn Den Vondel"), the man for
whom Vondelpark (Mission #3) is named.

Track down the armor display like the one below.

☐ IF YOU HAD TO GO TO BATTLE TO DEFEND MUIDER-
SLOT CASTLE, WHICH PIECES WOULD YOU CHOOSE **2**
TO WEAR? *POINTS*

Locate the old-fashioned costume display.

☐ HAVE YOUR PHOTO TAKEN **2**
POSING IN THE COSTUME *POINTS*
OF YOUR CHOICE.

☐ SNAP A PHOTO OF YOUR CASE
OFFICER(S) POSING **2**
IN ONE OF THE COSTUMES. *POINTS*

ANYTIME MISSIONS

THE BEST AGENTS HAVE A HIGH LEVEL OF SOMETHING CALLED "SITUATIONAL AWARENESS." THESE QUICK-WITTED AGENTS PAY CLOSE ATTENTION TO THEIR SURROUNDINGS – READY TO COLLECT CRITICAL INTELLIGENCE AND RESPOND TO DANGEROUS SITUATIONS. HAVING EXCELLENT "SITUATIONAL AWARENESS" (SA FOR SHORT) MEANS ALWAYS BEING "ON ALERT."

These missions will test your SA. Don't let your guard down as you wander around Amsterdam, or you may miss a chance to win points.

Amsterdam's Coat of Arms

Amsterdam's seal contains a red shield with three marks that appear like silver "Xs", but are actually angled crosses. An imperial crown and two lions surround a black stripe background which represents the Amstel River that flows through the city.

The motto at the bottom describes Amsterdam citizens during World War II: Valiant, Steadfast, Compassionate.

☐ ONE POINT FOR EVERY COAT-OF-ARMS YOU SPOT.

1 POINT EACH

TEN POINTS MAX

70+

- COAT OF ARMS
- EUROS
- WOODEN SHOES
- WINDMILLS
- BIKES & BOATS
- BRIDGES
- HOUSEBOATS
- HOUSES
- DUTCH FOOD
- SPEAKING DUTCH

Dutch Euros

The nations of the European Union share a currency, the euro. Each country personalizes its euros with national symbols. Locate euro coins to earn points for the next two clues.

☐ **WHO'S THE DUTCH KING ON THE EURO COIN?**

1 POINT

On coins made until 2013, this king's mother, a Dutch queen whose name starts with "B," appeared on the coins.

☐ **WHO'S THE DUTCH QUEEN ON THE EURO COIN?**

1 POINT

Souvenirs of Amsterdam

Three unofficial symbols of the Netherlands: wooden clogs, windmills, and tulips.

☐ **HAVE YOUR PHOTO SNAPPED TRYING ON WOODEN CLOGS.**

 2 POINTS

In centuries past, the Dutch relied on windmills to help clear the land of water (and to grind grain). Today, they make for a great "photo op."

☐ **HAVE YOUR PHOTO SNAPPED BESIDE A LARGE WINDMILL.** *Then...*

☑ **TRACK DOWN A MINIATURE WINDMILL IN A SOUVENIR SHOP.**

Amsterdam Transport

☐ **TAKE A SPIN ON AMSTERDAM'S TRANSPORT OF CHOICE: A BICYCLE.**

my notes:

_____

_____

☑ SPOT KIDS RIDING IN A "BAKFIET" (CARGO BIKE).

☐ TAKE A BOAT RIDE DOWN THE CITY'S CANALS.

☐ BONUS: "PEDAL" YOUR WAY DOWN THE CANALS AND DO A COMBO BOAT-AND-BIKE RIDE.

Amsterdam is filled with bridges - around 1300!

☐ **ONE POINT FOR EVERY *10* BRIDGES YOU SPOT.** **(20 POINTS MAX)**

While you're counting bridges, check out the houseboats lining the canals. How would you like to live on one of these?

Just as we have gardens for our homes, so do houseboats.

☑ **LOCATE A HOUSEBOAT WITH A GARDEN.**

☑ **BONUS: FIND A HOUSEBOAT WITH GRASS GROWING** **ON TOP.**

Amsterdam Houses

As Amsterdam's historic houses grow older, some
have begun to tilt as they settle. Keep a lookout
for these "lazy" houses that aren't standing up
straight.

☐ SNAP A PHOTO OF THE "LAZIEST" HOUSE YOU FIND **2** POINTS
  (A.K.A. THE MOST TILTED).

☐ BONUS: WHAT IS THE ADDRESS OF THIS HOUSE? **3** POINTS
(If you can't find the street number, the street
name is enough.)

Amsterdammers used to be taxed on the width of
their house. A sneaky way to get around paying
more taxes to the government: build your house up
instead of out. Keep a lookout for these "skinny"
houses.

2 POINTS

☐ SNAP A PHOTO OF THE "SKINNIEST" HOUSE YOU
  FIND.

3 POINTS

☐ BONUS: WHAT IS THE ADDRESS OF THIS HOUSE?
(If you can't find the street number, the street
name is enough.)

Dutch cheese is famous around the world, and the Netherlands even has a cheese museum. When you're at a restaurant or a market, venture beyond the typical cheddar cheese you may eat at home and try some Dutch favorites like Gouda ('how-dah') or Edam ('ay-dahm').

☐ **REPORT TO YOUR CASE OFFICER WHICH ONE SUITED YOUR TASTE AND WHICH ONE YOU FOUND THE MOST UNUSUAL.**

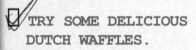

3
POINTS

The next two foods should please even the most "selective" (a.k.a. "pickiest") eaters.

☑ **TRY SOME DELICIOUS DUTCH WAFFLES.**

2
POINTS

Amsterdam serves up different types, including the gaufre ('go-fray') and stroopwafel ('strope-waffle').

☑ **TRY VLAAMSE FRITES ('VLAHM-SEH FREE-TES') (FRENCH FRIES).**

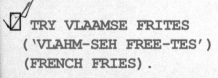

2
POINTS

The Dutch often eat their fries with mayonnaise or some other sauce (aside from ketchup). To earn points, try some sauce(s) other than ketchup.

ANYTIME MISSIONS: BONUS

COME ACROSS A MONUMENT OR EXHIBIT THAT'S CLOSED? NOT ENOUGH TIME IN THE CITY? HAVE NO FEAR, USE THESE MISSIONS TO ACHIEVE YOUR GOAL. YOUR CASE OFFICER SETS THE POINTS.

Blending in with your surroundings is critical for agents. One of the keys to blending in while visiting a foreign country: speaking the language. We won't expect you to magically become fluent in Dutch, but you will need to practice a few key phrases.

Put your skills to the test at, for example, restaurants and at your hotel.

____ POINTS FOR EACH OF THE BELOW SPOKEN TO A DIFFERENT DUTCH PERSON.

POINT(S) EACH

Hello = Hallo ("hah-low")

Hi = Hoi ("hoy")

Bye = **Dag** ("dah")

See you later = **Tot ziens** ("tote zeens")

Thank you = Dank u ("dhank-ew")

Thanks = Bedankt ("beh-dahnkt")

ANSWER KEY

Once an answer is submitted, your case officer can check it here. If you peek at this answer key before submitting a final answer, you won't receive any points for that clue. Most clues do not have one correct answer, for those that do, here are the answers.

#1 RIJKSMUSEUM -Javanese Men: A goes with 3; B goes with 1; C goes with 5; D goes with 2; E goes with 4; -Dutch East India Company Painting: Painted in 1665; the number of flags is the number YOU count (it's 15+). -'Night Watch', artist: Rembrandt; -The kids are teaching a cat to dance.; -The 'Merry Family' additions- window: a vase was added; Middle left side: the violin has an extra scroll on the left side (an extra "backwards 'J" design); Lower left side: a spoon was added in the pan; Right side chair (in front of the fire place): at the bottom, a third horizontal piece of wood was added; Middle, top of the cupboard: the vase on the left, an extra utensil was added

#2 VAN GOGH MUSEUM -The book: The Bible; -The name of the painting with the man and the potatoes: 'The Potato Eaters'; There are four people with him (5 total people).; -The 'Sunflowers' in the museum: D.; -The 'Bedroom' additions - The towel hanging on the wall: a red stripe was added. The painting hanging above the bed: another tree was added. On the table: a bottle was added on the right side.; -Monet's painting: 'Tulip Fields Near The Hague'.

#3 VONDELPARK -Vondel's resting place: Nieuwe kerk; -Picasso sculpture additions - The left side, the "fin"; a line was added. Bottom right: a circle was added. Top right "fin": a line was added.

#4 BEGIJNHOF -The year on the church: 1607

#5 DE DAM (National Monument) -The number of urns: 12

#7 HET SCHEEPVAARTMUSEUM -Directions in Dutch: Noord = North, Zuid = South, Oost = East, West = West

#10 ANYTIME -On euro coins, the king is Willem Alexander, the queen is Beatrix.

NOTE: the information in this book was accurate as of December 2014. We hope that you won't find anything outdated related to the clues. If you do find that something has changed, please email us at info@ScavengerHuntAdventures.com to kindly let us know.

THE FINAL MISSION

Case officers, please visit
scavengerhuntadventures.com/bonus
(all lowercase letters)

☐ JOIN 'THE INSIDER' (OUR EMAIL LIST)
You'll get a special bonus mission for
this city plus our free e-book,
The Museum Spy.

"I'm joining today!"

PLEASE HELP SPREAD THE WORD

We're a small family business and would be
thrilled if you **left a review online*** or
recommended our books to a friend.

"We'd Love To Help!"

OUR BOOKS
Paris, London, Amsterdam, Rome, New York,
D.C., Barcelona, St. Augustine – more on
the way!

*We can't mention the site name here, but it begins with "AM"!

GREAT FOR GROUP TRIPS

We offer **special multi-copy pricing** and **personalized
books** – great for field trips and group trips. Visit
scavengerhuntadventures.com/groups for more info.

IMAGE CREDITS
The two digit numbers are the file license number (links below), links to Flickr photographer sites are also below. License for all Flickr photos is Creative Commons 2.0.
(T=Top, B=Bottom, M=Middle; L=Left, R=Right, C=Center)

WIKIMEDIA: p.4:Tubs-3.0;p.5:T-Lencer-3.0;M-Avij-3.0;p.7-T-Heralder-3.0;p.13-Rijksmuseum;p.22-B-Ilaria-3.0;p.23-ML & MR: Guilhelm Vellut-3.0;p.24-T-Pemolo-3.0;p.25-B-Jo Jakeman-3.0;p.26:T-Bert K.-3.0;B-Brbbl-3.0;p.27:T-Archer10 (Dennis)-3.0;p.29-M-Nationaal Archives;B-Šarūnas Burdulis from USA-2.0;p.30-All:Deror_avi-3.0;p.34-BR-Arch-3.0;p.36&37 old photos:National Archives;p.39-T- Paalso Paal Sørensen-3.0;p.41-Eddo Hartmann-3.0;p.43-T-Holger Ellgaard-3.0;p.45-Pom2-3.0;p.46-Gamekeeper-3.0;p.52-Arch;p.53:BL-Haitham Alfalah;p.55:T-Bret-3.0;BL-Jorge Royan
FLICKR: p.28-Robert Scarth;p.29:T-Floris Looijesteijn;p.31-B-Downhilldom1984;p.35 All:Karl Baron;p.36:L-Luke Ma;p.38:L-Brodm (Drobm);R-David Berkowitz;p.40-Peter Krasznai;p.47-Sheila Anderson;p.48-Bertknot;p.50-B &p.51-BR-Ozz13x;p.51-BL-Eden Janine and Jim;p.53-TR-Chris Euromunzen;p.53-BR-Matthew Reid;p.54:TL-Rawdonfox;BL-Face Me Pls;BR-Kara Nagai;p.55 BR-Peter Corbett;p.56:TL-Fred Bigio;TR-Fabio Penna;BL-Randy Connolly;BR-Graeme Mclean;p.57:L-Andrij;M-James Grimmelmann;R-Word Junky;p.58:T-Updendra Kanda;B-Ryan Ready
Flickr User Links: Example: http://www.flickr.com/photos/79865753@N00 = 79865753@N00 ; Allie Caulfield: wm_archiv/; Andrij Bulba: andrijbulba/; Archer10 Dennis: photos/archer10/; Bertknot: photos/bertknot/; Chris Euromunzen: .8897024@N03/; David Berkowitz: davidberkowitz/; Drobm: /94645435@N00; Eden Janine Jim: edenpictures/; Fabio Penna: solapenna/; Face Me PLS: faceme/; Fred Bigio: bigiof/; Graeme Mclean: gee01/; Guilhelm Vellut: o_0/; Ilaria: 1la/; James Grimmelman: grimmelm/; Jo Jakeman: /76713068@N00; Kara Nagai: karanagai/; Luke Ma: lukema/; Matthew Reid: matthewreid/; Minister President Rutte: minister-president/; Ozz13x: 249310020@N02/; Peter Corbett: ptc24/; Peter Krasznai: kraszipeti/; Randolph Croft: rc_fotos/; Randy Connolly: randyconnolly/; Rawdonfox: 34739556@N04/; Rob Young: rob-young/; Robert Scarth: 18222776@N00/; Ryan Ready: ryanready/; Senan Sagsan: senan/; Upendra Kanda: ukanda/; Word Junky: wordjunky/
Additional Flickr User Links: Floris Looijesteijn : http://www.flickr.com/people/404889921@N05; Jo Jakeman: http://www.flickr.com/people/76713068@N00; Karl Baron: http://flickr.com/people/82365211@N00; Sheila Anderson: http://www.flickr.com/people/66691654@N00; Drobm: http://www.flickr.com/people/94645435@N00.

Links to Licenses:1.0: http://creativecommons.org/licenses/by-sa/1.0/deed.en; 1.2: creativecommons.org/licenses/by-sa/1.2/deed.en; 1.5: creativecommons.org/licenses/by-sa/1.5/deed.en;2.0: creativecommons.org/licenses/by-sa/2.0/deed.en; 2.5: creativecommons.org/licenses/by-sa/2.5/deed.en; 3.0: creativecommons.org/licenses/by-sa/3.0/deed.en

Lightning Source UK Ltd.
Milton Keynes UK
UKHW020618240419
341518UK00009B/89/P

9 780989 226707